The Cave

Written by
Rob Waring and **Maurice Jamall**

Before You Read

to drive (a boat)		shark's teeth	
to open		water (the sea)	
to push		cold	
boat		dark	
cave		heavy	
key		interesting	
lamp		old	
newspaper		wet	

80 years old

In the story

Faye

John

Tyler

David

Daniela

"What a great day," says John to his friends.
John, Daniela, Tyler, and David are in their boat.
Faye is driving the boat. Faye is good at driving boats.
"Let's go over there!" says Faye. "It looks interesting."
"Okay, let's go," says everybody.

Tyler sees something. He shows it to his friends. "Look, what's that?" he asks.

"Let's go and look," says John. "Is that a cave?" he asks.

Tyler says, "Yes. Wow! Let's go in."

They drive the boat to the cave.

They go into the cave. It is very dark.
"John, can you see?" asks Faye.
John says, "No, it's too dark. I can't see."
Daniela is worried. She doesn't like the dark cave.
"It's very dark. I don't want to go in," says Daniela.
"It's okay, Daniela," says Tyler.

But soon they can see. They get out of the boat
and look around the cave.
There are many interesting things in the cave.
There are some old books, lamps, and newspapers.
Faye sees something big.
"Wow!" says Faye. "Wow! Look at that!
What's that old thing?" she asks.
Tyler says, "I don't know.
But it's really interesting."

David sees something. "Hey, Daniela. What's this?" asks David.
He shows Daniela some shark's teeth.
Daniela says, "Stop that! David! Take it away!"
"Daniela, it's okay," says David.
"Why are these things in the cave?" asks John. "I think this is
somebody's cave. Somebody lives here."
"I don't think so," says Daniela. "These things are too old.
Nobody comes here now."

"Look at this newspaper," says Faye. "It's from 1979! It's really old!"

"Here are some more things. These are really interesting," says David. He shows Tyler some old things.

Tyler says, "This is a key. It looks really old. Why is it here?"

"I don't know," David says.

John sees an old bed. "Look at this old bed," John says. "It's great."

David shows Faye something. He asks, "What's this, Faye?"

"I don't know," she says. "But it's really great. I love this cave."

Daniela says, "But I don't like it. It's too dark in here. It's cold. Can we go?"

Daniela and David look at the boat and the water.
"Oh, no! Look!" says Daniela. "The water's coming in!"
"Let's get out," says David. He gets into the boat.
David and Daniela want to get out of the cave.
"We can't get out!" says David.

The water is high now. The boat cannot get out of the cave. David says, "We can't get out of the cave! What can we do?" "Oh no!" says Daniela again. "Where can we get out?" she asks.
"Daniela, it's okay," says Faye.
"Wait! It's okay. Don't worry, Daniela," says John. "The water doesn't come up to here. See? These things are not wet."

Tyler isn't worried. He looks around the cave.
Tyler sees something. He tells everyone. "Look!
We can get out of here. We can go this way."
"Great!" says Faye. "Let's go."
"You go first, John," says Faye.
"Next, Daniela can go, then David, Tyler, and me,"
she says.

Daniela and John get to the top.
John says, "Hey, everybody, there's a door! We can get out! But it looks heavy."
The door is too heavy and very old. He cannot open it. He pushes the door, but it does not open. "Oh, no! We can't get out," John says.
Everyone is worried now.

"I can't open it," says John. "I don't have the key."
"Oh no. I can help," says Daniela. She helps John.
They push the door.
"Push, Daniela," says John. But the door does not open.
David goes up to them. He has the old key.
"Daniela, is this the key?" David asks.

David gives the key to Daniela. She puts the key in the door.

"It's very heavy," says John. "Help me, Daniela."

"Let's push," she says. They push the door open.

"It's open!" says John. "We can get out."

"Come on, everybody," says Daniela. She is happy. She can get out now.

Everybody gets out of the cave. They are not worried now.
"I like it here," says John. "This cave is great. Let's come back tomorrow and get the boat."
"You can. But not me!" says Daniela. "I'm not coming back!"
John smiles at Daniela. Daniela smiles back.